LUKE'S GOLF DISCOVERY

By
Xuemei Ding

Published by D&D Concordia LLC

Luke's Golf Discovery

Copyright © 2025 by Xuemei Ding
All rights reserved.
No part of this book may be reproduced, distributed, or transmitted in any form or by any means, including electronic, mechanical, photocopying, recording, or by any information storage and retrieval system, without prior written permission from the publisher, except for brief quotations in reviews or for educational purposes as permitted by law.

Published by D&D Concordia LLC
Charlottesville, Virginia

ISBN: 979-8-218-63251-9

This book is inspired by real-life experiences but ultimately a work of fiction. Certain characters, places, and events have been fictionalized for storytelling purposes.

This Book Belongs to:

This book is dedicated to my son, Lucas Dunaway, whose love for golf and invaluable inspiration brought this story to life.

Luke's Golf Discovery

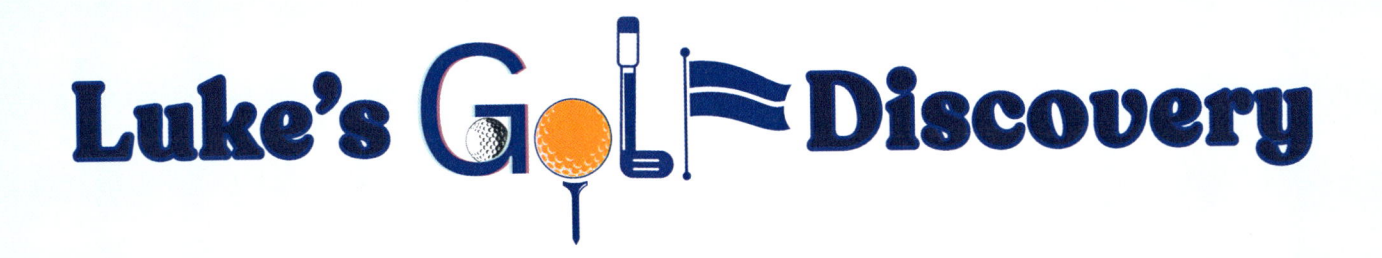

By
Xuemei Ding

Published by D&D Concordia LLC

Luke was always a quiet kid, except when he was with his Labrador Retriever, Birdee. At home, he would tell Birdee stories while scratching behind his ears or play soccer with him in the backyard.

But at school? While other kids ran across the soccer field or dribbled basketballs, Luke sat on a bench by the monkey bars, twisting his colorful 3x3 Rubik's cube. Click, twist, turn—SOLVED.

Sometimes, he would watch other kids play from a distance. But join in? No way! He wasn't the fastest. He wasn't the strongest. And what if they laughed at him when he made mistakes?

Green Frog Elementary School

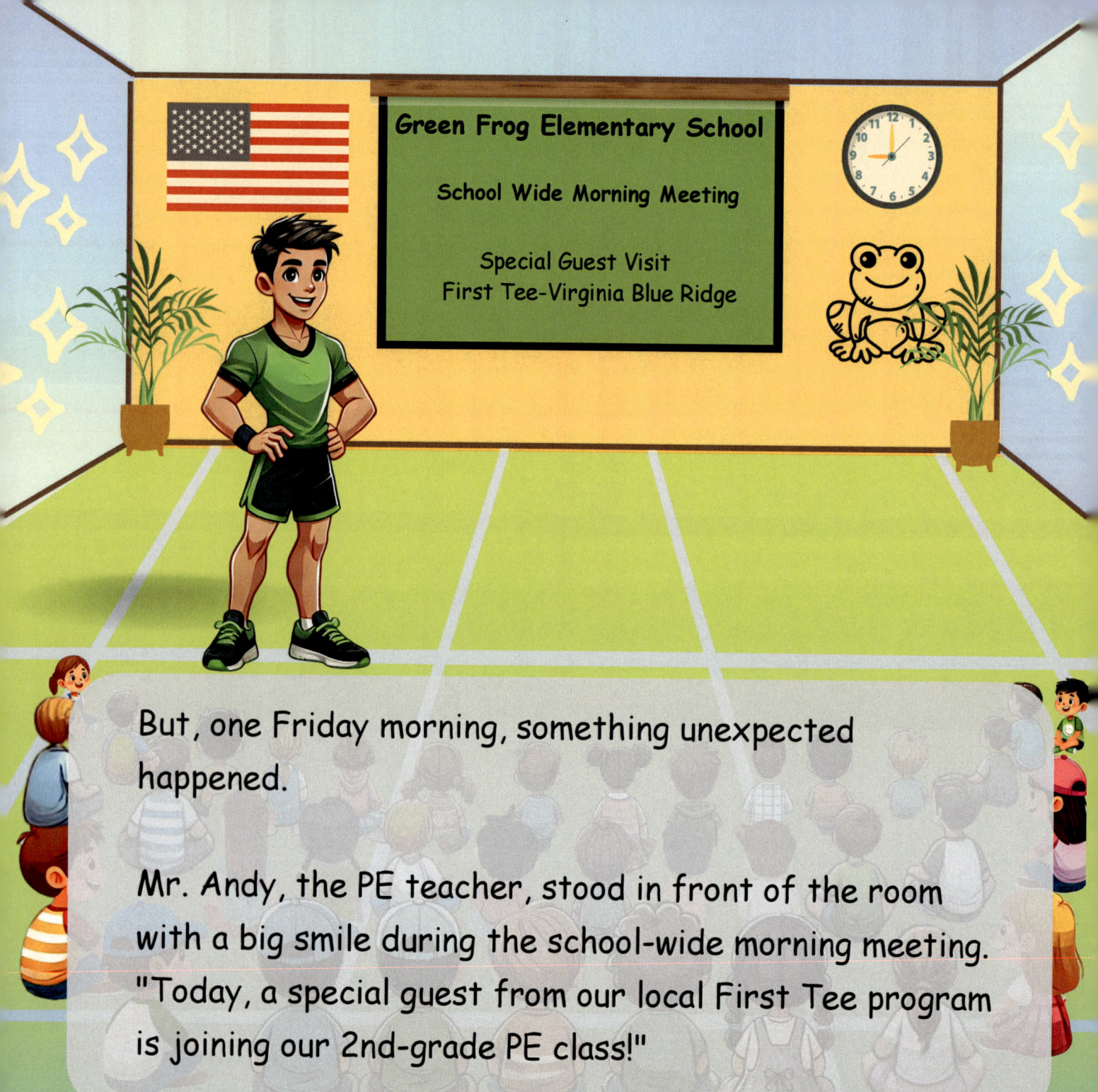

School Wide Morning Meeting

Special Guest Visit
First Tee-Virginia Blue Ridge

But, one Friday morning, something unexpected happened.

Mr. Andy, the PE teacher, stood in front of the room with a big smile during the school-wide morning meeting. "Today, a special guest from our local First Tee program is joining our 2nd-grade PE class!"

Jacob raised his hand. "What's First Tee?"

"Great question, Jacob!"

Mr. Andy smiled. "First Tee is a youth program where kids learn to play golf while also developing good habits such as being honest, staying confident, never giving up, and so much more."

Excitement filled the room.

Soccer: 5 > 3 WIN
Basketball: 69 > 60 WIN

BUT in Golf?
72 > 80 WIN
MAKES NO SENSE....

Luke knew very little about golf—the lower the score, the better. He always thought that was backwards. In football or soccer, winning was determined by scoring more goals. In basketball, more points were better, too. But in golf? Less was more. It didn't make sense. But something about Mr. Andy's announcement sparked Luke's curiosity.

After lunch, Luke and his classmates rushed outside for PE class. Mr. Andy was talking to a tall man in a white collared shirt tucked into his khaki pants. A few golf bags stood nearby, and a giant green carpet-like mat stretched like a putt-putt course.

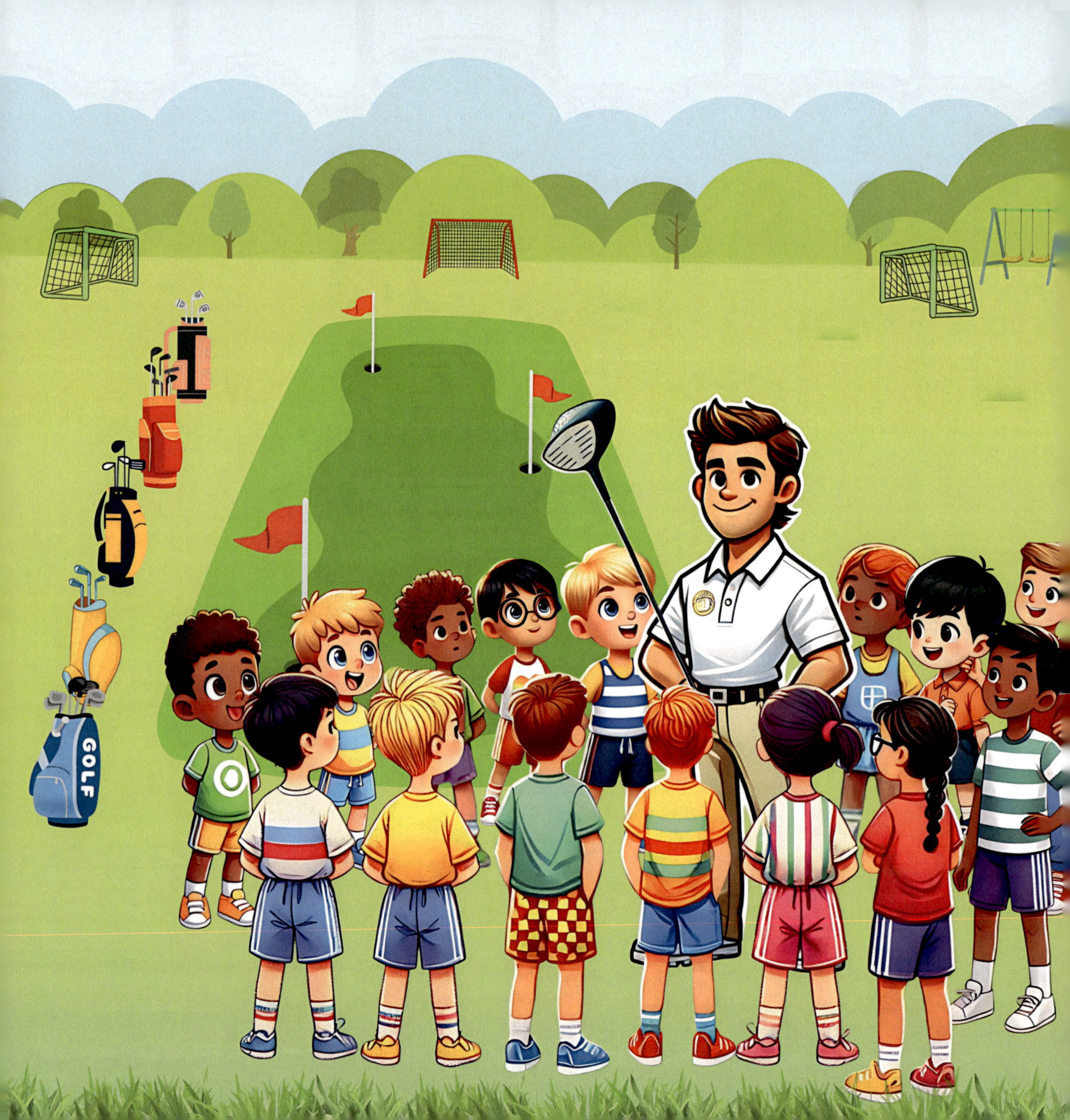
GOLF

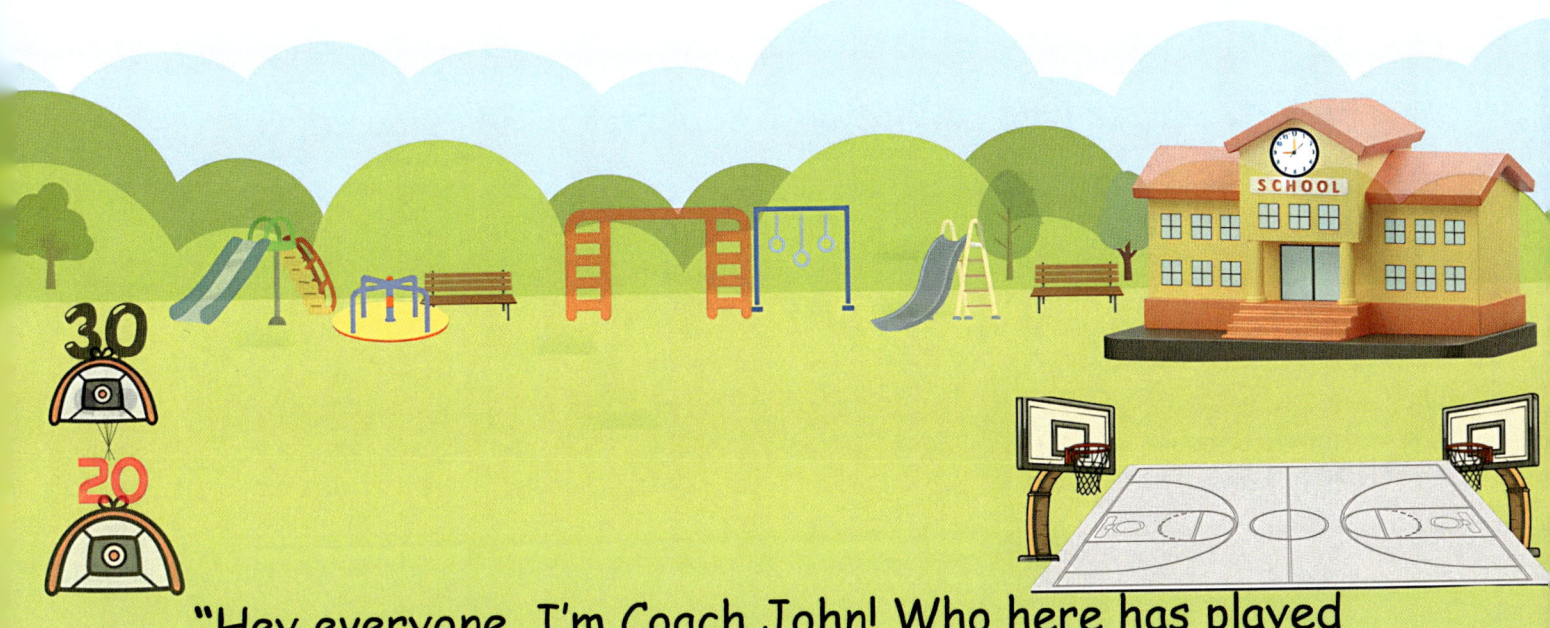

"Hey everyone, I'm Coach John! Who here has played golf?"

No one raised their hands.

"No worries!" said Coach John. "First, let me tell you what makes golf unique compared to many other sports. Golf isn't about speed or strength. Anyone can play golf." He continued. "Okay. Let's go over the equipment we need to play the game—golf clubs! Like people, each club has unique personality and identity!"

He pulled out a long club with a giant head. "This is a driver. Think of the driver as the golf superhero. It is powerful, commanding, and gets all attention."

"Driver? Like the driver of a car?" Luke asked as he tilted his head in confusion.

Coach John laughed. "Exactly! Like a car on the highway, the driver speeds your ball down the fairway with a powerful swing."

Then he reached for another club with a flat, slightly angled face. "This one is called an iron. It is like a Swiss Army knife; The iron is used to tackle many different kinds of shots."

Finally, he grabbed a short shaft with a flat and wide clubhead. "And this is a putter. The putter is like the chess master of the golf bag. A putter is not about power; it is all about precision."

Luke's eyes widened as he looked at all the clubs. Golf was way more interesting than he expected. Unlike sports that emphasized speed or strength, this sport required skill and precision, which immediately captured his curiosity.

The first game was tic-tac-toe with putters! The class was divided into two teams. Luke watched Jacob and Katie play rock-paper-scissors to decide which team would go first. "Rock, paper, scissors—shoot!" Jacob threw the rock, and Katie had scissors. "No! My scissors got crushed!" Katie gasped dramatically.

Grinning, Jacob positioned himself for the first putt, but he hit too hard. The ball rolled past the grid. "Oops!"

Katie tried next but barely tapped the ball. It stopped too soon.

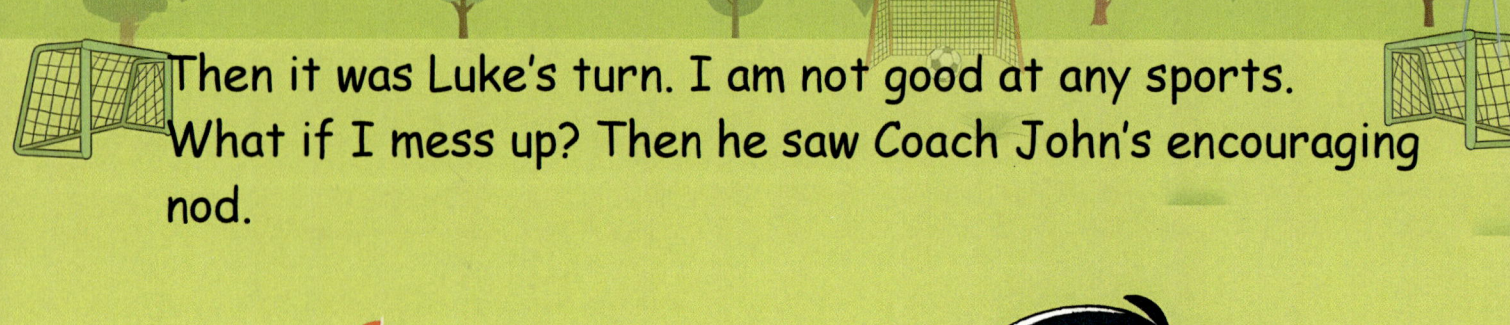

Then it was Luke's turn. I am not good at any sports. What if I mess up? Then he saw Coach John's encouraging nod.

"Tick-tock. The ball rolled across the mat smoothly and stopped perfectly in the center square.

"Whoa!" Katie cheered, giving him a high-five.

Did I just do that? Luke felt a small, warm confidence inside. For the first time in PE class, kids were cheering for him.

Coach John clapped his hands together as the tic-tac-toe game ended. "Excellent work, everyone! This time, let's try something more challenging!"

Coach John continued, pointing to three nets placed at different distances. "Your goal? Chipping the ball into the air and landing it as close to the target as possible!"

Charlie went first. He swung hard and completely missed. SWOOSH! The ball didn't move. Laughter filled the air.

Then it was Luke's turn. Luke positioned the club and made a gentle swing. The ball lifted off the ground and landed right into the middle chipping net.

"You make it look way too easy!" Charlie fist-pumped with Luke.

Luke quietly thanked him with a warm smile. He felt a sense of pride in his achievement.

Coach John clapped his hands once more. "All right, fantastic work on the chipping, too. Now it's time for the most exciting part." Holding the driver up, he continued, "Let's hit some balls with our superhero club."

"You want your feet to be somewhat wider than your shoulders. Line up the ball just inside your front foot. Hold the club firmly but keep your grip relaxed as if you're shaking hands."

Luke gripped the driver, but when he swung—whoosh! He totally missed the ball. A few kids giggled. A glimmer of doubt crept in. Everyone will laugh if I fail again...

"Relax, Luke. Swing it smoothly. Let the club do the work."

Luke adjusted his stance. He took a deep breath, pulled the driver back, and swung through the ball, extending his arms and sending the ball flying.

"Whoa! I did it!" he shouted. Cheers broke out.

Luke was already captivated by the game of golf.

At the end of the class, Coach John handed each student a golf ball. "Take this home with you, and remember what we learned today. Again, golf is a game for everyone. If you keep working hard and love the game, every swing will get you closer to something exciting and new. And one day you may be playing in a real tournament!"

Playing in a real golf tournament? Luke had never thought about it. But now with a golf ball in his hands, it didn't seem so impossible.

That night, Luke lay in bed, rolling the golf ball in his hands. "You know what, Birdee? I think I really like golf." Luke whispered to Birdee.

Luke felt a new kind of excitement rising within him and finally drifted off to sleep.

In his dream, he was no longer just a puzzle-solving kid. He was Luke, the golfer.

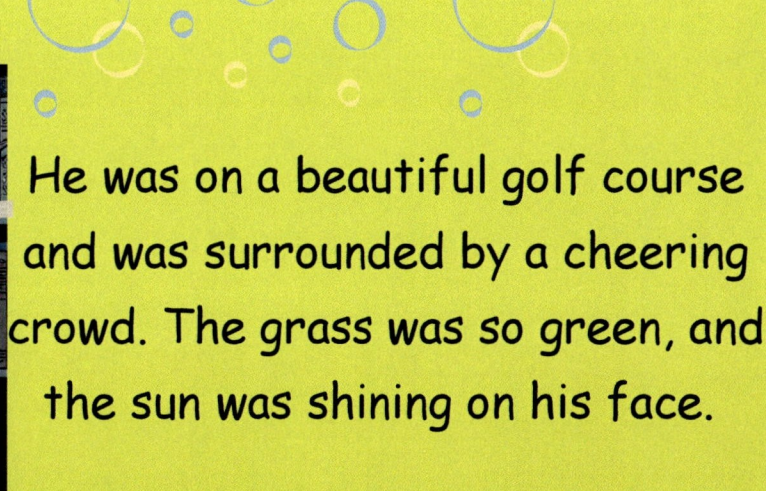

He was on a beautiful golf course and was surrounded by a cheering crowd. The grass was so green, and the sun was shining on his face.

He would win the tournament with a final stroke. Tick-Tock. He rocked the putter. The ball rolled on the green... closer... closer...until it disappeared into the hole!

Birdee was next to him and gave a small bark. Luke woke up from his dream. Luke gave his pup a scratch behind his ears. "You're right, buddy. I think I should start practicing golf first, right?"

Luke tucked the ball under his pillow, wondering if this is the start of his golf adventure.

From that day on, golf became Luke's passion — he didn't have to be the fastest or the strongest. All he had to do was be himself, have fun, and be ready to welcome the next challenge!

Acknowledgment

I want to express my gratitude to everyone who helped me bring this story to life. A special thanks to my son Lucas, whose own golf journey helped shape the story and added a personal and relatable touch. Equally, I extend my deepest appreciation to his coach, Mark Marshall, for his patience, mentorship, and unwavering belief in Lucas.

I am also grateful to our local First Tee chapter, First Tee-Virginia Blue Ridge, for its dedication to teaching kids patience, confidence, and other vital life qualities through the game of golf. Although the story mentions First Tee, please note that the book is neither affiliated with nor endorsed by First Tee.

Finally, loving thanks to my husband for your constant support and encouragement throughout this project. It has meant so much to me that you believed in me.

Made in the USA
Middletown, DE
04 April 2025